Sports in America

Look for these and other books in the Lucent Overview series:

Sports in America

by Sarah Flowers

LUCENT
BOOKS

Library of Congress Cataloging-in-Publication Data

Flowers, Sarah, 1952–
    Sports in America / by Sarah Flowers.
       p. cm. — (Lucent overview series)
    Includes bibliographical references (p.) and index.
    Summary: Describes the important role of sports in American
society, business, entertainment, and schools.
    ISBN 1-56006-178-2 (alk. paper)
    1. Sports—Social aspects—United States.   [1. Sports.]
    I. Title.   II. Series.
    GV706.5.F56   1996
    306.4'83'0973—dc20

96-3430
CIP
AC

Copyright © 1996 by Lucent Books, Inc.
P.O. Box 289011, San Diego, CA 92198-9011
Printed in the U.S.A.

Contents

PEANUTS
.90

Introduction

AMERICANS LOVE SPORTS and hail athletic achievement. They admire the strength of a boxer like Riddick Bowe, marvel at the speed of a football player like Deion Sanders, treasure the grace of a basketball player like Michael Jordan, wonder at the versatility of a heptathlete like Jackie Joyner-Kersee, and prize the dedication and endurance of a baseball player like Cal Ripken Jr. They revel in the excitement of competition and the thrill of victory. Even in the face of defeat, Americans take satisfaction in knowing the competitors have done their absolute best.

Americans by the millions show their appreciation for sports as both participants and devoted fans. At any time of year, weekend or weekday, parks and gymnasiums across the nation teem with youth and adult sports leagues and individuals playing pickup games. Fans fill stadiums, arenas, tracks, courts, and greens or pile up in front of television sets to watch their favorite athletes or teams. "Surveys indicate that nearly 75 percent of Americans participate in, watch, read about, or talk about sport with others on a daily basis," writes sociology professor Jay Coakley.

Well-known athletes, rightly or not, are heroes and role models, celebrities and entertainers, and the sports to which they devote themselves are

(Opposite page) Fans pack a stadium to watch the action of a professional baseball game. With an overwhelming majority of Americans involved in sports, either as fans or participants, it is evident that sports are a large part of American culture.

7

not mere pastimes. They are a central part of American life. Coakley writes, "Sport makes up a significant part of our news coverage, and it is often an important part of family lives, our educational experiences, our economy and our political system, and even our religious life."

Reflections of society

In many ways, sport reflects American society. Changes in attitudes toward women and minorities on the playing field, for example, have paralleled changes in society. Violence on the field and

Americans embrace the achievements of well-known athletes such as Dallas Cowboys quarterback Troy Aikman.

in the stands, lack of respect for rules and refer-
ees, and an emphasis on winning over sportsmanship can also be seen as reflections of an America
that today agonizes over a decline in civil behavior and moral values. As University of Utah history professor Larry Gerlach stated in a speech
several years ago, "Sport accurately reflects
American society, its frustrations, its fantasies, its
cultural values. The arena is at once apart from
and a part of everyday life."

*Young fans eagerly await an
autograph from baseball star
Cal Ripkin Jr. Americans look to
famous athletes as heroes and
role models.*

1

Athletics or Big Business?

IN AMERICA TODAY, sports mean big money. Star athletes earn salaries well into the millions and professional sports teams are valued in the hundreds of millions. Product endorsements, in which athletes lend their names and faces to companies selling products ranging from shoes to soft drinks to cars, add millions more to the annual earnings of big-name athletes. The combined salary and endorsement earnings of basketball's Michael Jordan, for example, totaled $43.9 million in 1995, according to estimates by *Forbes* magazine. Boxer Mike Tyson earned $40 million in 1995, with just over half that amount coming from one fight that lasted eighty-nine seconds. Salary and endorsements put football's Deion Sanders, basketball's Shaquille O'Neal, and boxing's Riddick Bowe near the $20 million mark, followed closely by boxer George Foreman, golfer Jack Nicklaus, and tennis player Andre Agassi.

The big money doesn't all go to the athletes. In hopes of earning handsome profits, television networks pay huge sums of money to broadcast major sporting events such as the Olympics. NBC, for example, paid more than $400 million to the International Olympic Committee (IOC) to tele-

(Opposite page) Race cars bear the logos of corporate sponsors. Increasingly, professional sports rely on big business for their existence.

vise the Summer Olympic Games in 1992. Professional sports leagues annually take in billions of dollars for broadcasting rights alone. According to one writer, the National Football League (NFL) earned $40 million per team from television revenues in 1993, while major league baseball's 1993 television revenues totaled $1.5 billion.

"Sports is not simply another big business," writes Michael Ozanian of *Financial World* magazine. "It is one of the fastest-growing industries in the U.S., and it is intertwined with virtually every aspect of the economy—from media and apparel to food and advertising."

The Chicago Bulls' Michael Jordan pulls down a rebound during a 1995 playoff game against the Orlando Magic. Jordan's earnings of close to $44 million—mostly from product endorsements—made him the highest paid athlete of 1995.

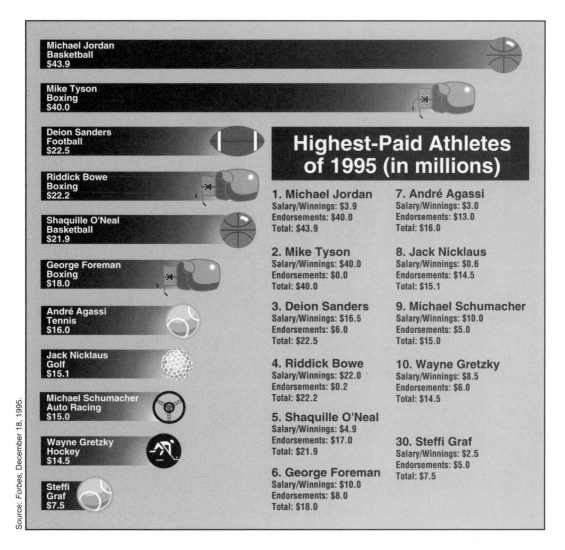

Michael Jordan
Basketball
$43.9

Mike Tyson
Boxing
$40.0

Deion Sanders
Football
$22.5

Riddick Bowe
Boxing
$22.2

Shaquille O'Neal
Basketball
$21.9

George Foreman
Boxing
$18.0

André Agassi
Tennis
$16.0

Jack Nicklaus
Golf
$15.1

Michael Schumacher
Auto Racing
$15.0

Wayne Gretzky
Hockey
$14.5

Steffi
Graf
$7.5

Source: *Forbes*, December 18, 1995.

Highest-Paid Athletes of 1995 (in millions)

1. Michael Jordan
Salary/Winnings: $3.9
Endorsements: $40.0
Total: $43.9

2. Mike Tyson
Salary/Winnings: $40.0
Endorsements: $0.0
Total: $40.0

3. Deion Sanders
Salary/Winnings: $16.5
Endorsements: $6.0
Total: $22.5

4. Riddick Bowe
Salary/Winnings: $22.0
Endorsements: $0.2
Total: $22.2

5. Shaquille O'Neal
Salary/Winnings: $4.9
Endorsements: $17.0
Total: $21.9

6. George Foreman
Salary/Winnings: $10.0
Endorsements: $8.0
Total: $18.0

7. André Agassi
Salary/Winnings: $3.0
Endorsements: $13.0
Total: $16.0

8. Jack Nicklaus
Salary/Winnings: $0.6
Endorsements: $14.5
Total: $15.1

9. Michael Schumacher
Salary/Winnings: $10.0
Endorsements: $5.0
Total: $15.0

10. Wayne Gretzky
Salary/Winnings: $8.5
Endorsements: $6.0
Total: $14.5

30. Steffi Graf
Salary/Winnings: $2.5
Endorsements: $5.0
Total: $7.5

Games, matches, and meets are no longer just a chance to see some rousing action, honest competition, and talented players. They are a commercial enterprise, a place for sponsors and advertisers to snare new customers. Today, sport is big business. As David Guterson writes in *Harper's Magazine*:

> Arenas and the vast perimeters of stadiums are thoroughly festooned with advertisements and big-screen graphics that fans can neither ignore nor turn away from: the scoreboard, the game clock,

the scorer's bench, the chairs where NBA [National Basketball Association] players rest, the shirts and sweatpants worn by ball boys, the cups players drink from and the towels around their necks—even the shoes they wear on their feet—are chockablock with sales messages.

The relationship between sport and business isn't entirely new, however. In 1953, when August Busch of the Busch beer brewing family gained a controlling interest in the St. Louis Cardinals baseball team, "the Cardinals were quickly transformed into a traveling billboard for the brewery," write Busch biographers Peter Hernon and Terry Ganey.

Who benefits?

Of course, business isn't the only party to benefit from the relationship between business and sport. Such sports as tennis, golf, and car racing rely heavily on corporate sponsorship to survive. Often, companies pay for equipment and put up prize money in exchange for prominent display of the company name or logo. Without that support many sporting events might not take place at all.

Increasingly, professional sports teams play in stadiums and arenas built with money from corporations rather than public funds.

The Colorado Rockies, for example, play in a new stadium called Coors Field, after the brewing company that helped to build it. The Utah Jazz play in the Delta Center, built with help from Delta Airlines; the Los Angeles Lakers play in the Great Western Forum, named for Great Western Bank, and the Washington Bullets and Capitols play in the USAir Arena, built with help from USAir. In exchange for $500,000 to upgrade Candlestick Park in San Francisco in time for the 1999 Super Bowl, 3Com Corporation got the

Members of America 3 *defend the America's Cup title in 1995. Their sailboat boldly displays the names of the companies that pay for much of their training and competitions.*

An outfielder is dwarfed by an immense advertisement that covers part of the back wall of a ballpark.

right to rename the 49ers' home field 3Com Park, at least for home games during the 1995 season.

Some fans see no problem with this type of sponsorship. The San Jose *Mercury-News* asked readers how they felt about Candlestick's conversion to 3Com Park. Fan Maggie Goeppner faced the reality: "I will call it 3Com Park. The city really needs the money, and if they didn't get the Super Bowl, I think everyone would complain." Timothy Chui agreed, "It isn't wrong to name a park after a company when the company is willing to fund the development that benefits all people."

But other fans feel that changing a name is going too far. "It's a shame money always has to rule over tradition," said Terry Stevens. "Let 3Com get credit in its own way through advertising. Why do they have to change everything?" Another fan offered this view:

It will always be Candlestick to me. It tells me everything is for sale. These teams wonder why there's no fan loyalty any more. It's because anything and everybody is up for sale nowadays. It's disgusting.

The role of television

The business world's influence on sports stems largely from the presence of television. Television has the ability to connect millions of viewers—and, more importantly, consumers—with companies that have something to sell. In 1948, before most households had a television, people could follow sports only through the limited media of radio and print. To see a game, you had to be there, translating into much smaller audiences for advertisers. During the entire 1948 season, for example, twenty-one million people were able to

A television camera captures the excitement of a professional football game. Television serves as the main connection between corporate sponsors and consumers.

see baseball games by going to ballparks. In contrast, the final game of the 1991 World Series alone attracted ninety million television viewers.

Surveys show that sports continue to attract large numbers of viewers. A 1993 study revealed that 50 percent of American men and 28 percent of American women watch professional football on television. In addition, large numbers of television sports watchers are young and educated—exactly the audience advertisers want to reach. "No sport, except perhaps polo, can survive these days without television coverage. . . . Without TV, the most important link between sponsors and their target audience would be lost," says *Financial World* magazine.

Pleasing the television audience

Sports teams and leagues are well aware of the importance of television, and they have been eager to adapt to its needs even when that means changing the way a game is played. For example, professional football introduced the two-minute warning, a stopping point near the end of each half, to allow time for advertisements. Professional baseball added more time-outs to its game, also to allow advertisers more opportunities to reach the viewing public.

Rule changes have also been made in hopes of spicing up games for television viewers. Professional football added the two-point conversion for this purpose, according to sportswriter Skip Rozin. The two-point conversion allows a team to earn two extra points after a touchdown by passing or running the ball into the end zone rather than taking the usual point-after kick that earns one extra point. The NFL added the two-point conversion because it realized that "scoring makes fans happy," and happy fans make a special effort to watch games, Rozin writes.

Television has even influenced changes in game times. "Games in all sports now start at hours of the day and night determined by the television networks in conjunction with the leagues, and play often is halted at the discretion of officials who call time-outs for commercials," writes David Guterson.

Major sports events such as playoff and championship games are almost always played at times determined by the television networks. In most cases, this means during television's prime-time evening hours from 8 P.M. to 11 P.M. Thus, games played on the East Coast might start as late as 9 P.M.—still in prime time, but late enough to allow West Coast viewers time to get home from work to watch the 6 P.M. game. Because the television audience is larger during prime-time hours, weekday games—once the norm in baseball—are almost unheard-of during playoff season today.

Jerry Gorman and Kirk Calhoun, authors of *The Name of the Game: The Business of Sports*, believe that this approach to scheduling of sports events may eventually deprive sports of fans by "sacrific[ing] anybody who cannot stay up till 11 P.M. in the East to watch a game." They continue:

> Consider baseball. Baseball is a sport with a pattern of attracting its fans young and holding onto them despite the lure of faster and flashier sports. It has not been as hard for those young fans to watch baseball on television since the network's earliest days of broadcasting. "What they have done is write off an entire generation of Americans," according to Curt Smith in *Voices in the Game.*

Today, few deny that athletics and big business go hand in hand. Professional sports, in particular, have "gained recognition as a vital part of the burgeoning [growing] mass-entertainment industry," one writer notes. The ties between business and sport are likely to grow stronger in the future.

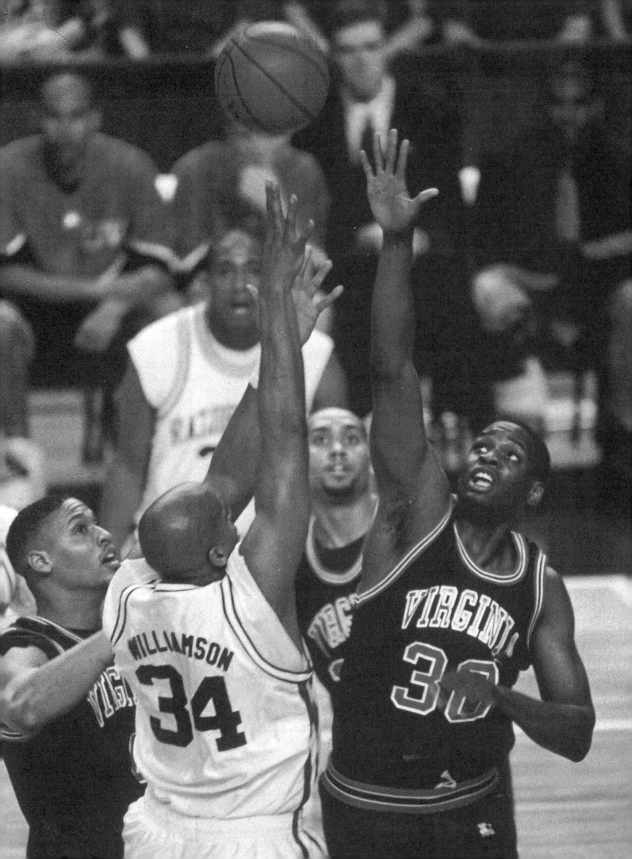

2

Sports and Studies: An Uneasy Alliance

IN THE UNITED STATES, almost three hundred thousand young men and women participate in college sports of all types. College football and basketball, especially, entertain millions of fans each year, both in person and on television. Yet many people question whether sports belong on college campuses at all. They maintain that college studies and college athletics are both full-time activities, and that no one can do both well. Supporters of college sports point to successful student-athletes, like Steve Young, who graduated from Brigham Young University and went on to law school while playing football. They point out schools like Indiana University and Notre Dame, which turn out top teams year after year while maintaining high academic standards for their athletes.

College athletic programs are a vital part of most American college campuses. They generate money and build school spirit. But a growing number of people believe that college sports as they exist today do not serve the best interests of athletes, other students, or the schools them-

(Opposite page) Players battle for control of the ball at the start of a college basketball game. Many have criticized college athletics as being incompatible with a college's academic purpose.

21

selves. These critics propose some major changes in the way college athletics are run.

The route to the pros

For some athletes, college is the only route to professional sports. Hoping a successful college athletic career will earn them a place on a professional team, some young athletes go to college, but not to study. Football coach Jim Walden of Iowa State University says that "not more than 20% of the football players go to college for an education. And that may be a high figure."

Pro football and basketball recruit new players almost exclusively from college teams, so they monitor the progress of promising young athletes. Players rely on games as a showcase for their talents. Even professional hockey and baseball, which have training and recruiting systems independent of the colleges, have instituted college drafts, making higher education a stepping-stone into these sports as well.

Most athletes who enter college with the primary purpose of reaching the NFL or NBA are willing to put massive amounts of time and energy into their sports. They may care little about what college has to offer them other than training, playing time, and exposure in their sport. Critics suggest that these athletes would be ideal candidates for a minor league system in which they could receive all of those things without the expectation that they be college students as well. Because there is no minor league system, they end up in college, often planning to stay only long enough to get a professional contract. When they see college as only one step on the path to a professional contract, class attendance becomes secondary. Deion Sanders, who signed a contract with the Atlanta Falcons of the NFL without graduating from Florida State University, was one of those who attended class as little as possible. When asked whether he wanted to be in college, he replied, "No, but I have to be."

Few young hopefuls will actually make the pros. A recent survey by the NCAA (National Collegiate Athletic Association) President's Commission showed that more than 23 percent of college athletes and 44 percent of black college athletes think that they have a good chance to make the pros. But of the almost sixty-three thousand young men playing college football and basketball, fewer than two hundred (less than 1

Some student-athletes, such as former Brigham Young University football player Steve Young, are able to successfully combine college sports and academics.

percent) will ever play ball professionally, and even fewer will make a career of it. Still, they dream. As sports psychologist Thomas Tutko says, "There's nothing wrong with having those dreams. It's when you sacrifice everything else that the problem occurs."

Student-athletes or athlete-students?

The main thing sacrificed is schoolwork. Student-athletes are expected to do two things: perform for their team and study toward a degree completion. The two often do not work together very well. Athletes spend hours each day practicing, attending team meetings, watching game films, working out with weights, and running. After all that, some athletes barely have the energy to attend class, much less do another three or four hours of homework. As one former college basketball player said of his days as a student-athlete:

> It was all you could do to drag yourself back to the dorm each day. By the time you ate and got back to your room, it was 8:30, and all you could think about was getting your weary bones in bed and getting some sleep. Who had time to study?

In some cases, students manage to combine their sports skills with their academic goals. Former University of Virginia basketball player Ralph Sampson refused to turn professional before completing his college degree. Tennis champion Arthur Ashe said of Sampson, "It would have been well worth it to him to borrow money to attend a school like the University of Virginia. . . . He decided to 'use' Virginia to market his basketball skills while attending classes." And there are dozens of unheralded players like Mike Atkinson of Long Beach State University, who will never play in the NBA, but who used his basketball scholarship to earn a degree in criminology and law enforcement.

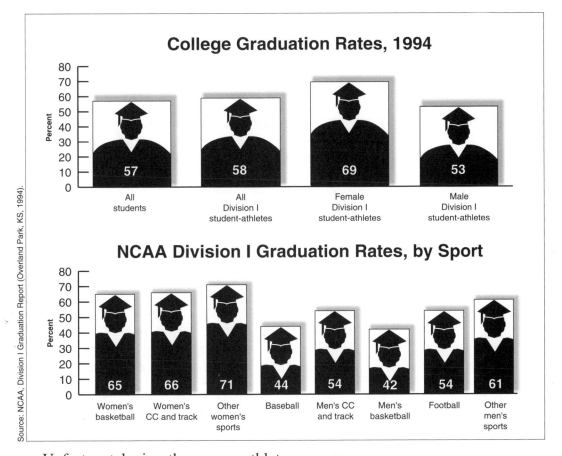

College Graduation Rates, 1994

	All students	All Division I student-athletes	Female Division I student-athletes	Male Division I student-athletes
Percent	57	58	69	53

NCAA Division I Graduation Rates, by Sport

	Women's basketball	Women's CC and track	Other women's sports	Baseball	Men's CC and track	Men's basketball	Football	Other men's sports
Percent	65	66	71	44	54	42	54	61

Source: NCAA, Division I Graduation Report (Overland Park, KS, 1994).

Unfortunately, in other cases, athletes emerge from college with no education and no job. In the 1980s, twenty-three-year-old Kevin Ross made national headlines when he enrolled in elementary school. He had played basketball for Creighton University for four years, but he could barely read and write. By the time Ross left the university he was only thirty-two units short of receiving a degree. He managed to get that far by taking nonacademic classes such as ceramics and first aid and because coaches, teachers, and others cared more about his basketball skills than about helping him learn. Athletes like Ross, who are not selected by professional teams, are often lost, with no job skills and no education. Tom Sanders, former Boston Celtic star, says:

I remember when a high draft pick was cut from the Celtics one year, and he sat in front of his locker with his head down crying out, "what am I going to do now?" The young man did not have a college degree, and without basketball felt completely lost. I was to see this scene repeated many times during my career as a player and coach.

Are NCAA rules fair to athletes?

How do athletes get to college in the first place if they are unprepared to do college work? Colleges compete to recruit the best high school athletes, even if those athletes are not the best students academically. Recruiting rules are set by the National Collegiate Athletic Association (NCAA). Some critics complain that the NCAA rules are too generous, admitting students who would not be eligible under academic requirements alone, and failing to require athletes to perform to their full scholastic potential. Others complain that the rules are too strict, denying admission to young athletes who could benefit from college, but whose background didn't prepare them for it. And some maintain that athletes perform no worse academically than students as a whole at most colleges.

All colleges have some basis for admitting students. Most use a combination of high school grades, test scores, essays, and interviews. Some are highly selective, admitting only a small percentage of those who apply; others admit nearly anyone with a high school diploma. Most colleges hope that their students will be a varied group, with different interests and abilities. Therefore, even the most selective do not simply accept applicants with the highest grades and test scores; they also want people with backgrounds and active interests in such areas as art, politics, music, journalism, community and cultural volunteer work, and sports.

In the past, some colleges virtually ignored admissions standards when it came to athletes. Kevin Ross entered Creighton University in 1978 with a score of 9 out of a possible 36 on the ACT (American College Testing) exam. That year, the average score for entering Creighton students was 23.2. Not long after Ross's story was made public, the NCAA adopted new, stiffer admissions requirements, known as Proposition 48. Under the new rules, an incoming freshman had to have a high school average of C in eleven core courses (including English, math, and science) in order to play a sport at any NCAA Division I or IA school. He or she also had to score at least 700 on the combined math and verbal portions of the Scholastic Aptitude Test (SAT) or a composite score of 15 on the ACT. Freshmen who did not meet these requirements could still be awarded athletic scholarships, but could not play until they had shown that they could do college-level schoolwork. Proposition 48 was later modified to state that athletes who did not meet the academic requirements could not receive athletic scholarships. In 1996, the requirements became even stricter, requiring a minimum grade point average GPA of 2.5 (C+) in thirteen core courses and a score of 820 on the SAT-I or 17.5 on the ACT.

Too strict or not strict enough?

These requirements, although less stringent than the requirements for nonathletes at most colleges, are difficult for many prospective athletes. The documentary *Hoop Dreams*, which follows the lives of two Chicago high school basketball stars, dramatizes this situation: Central character William Gates has to take the ACT five times before he manages to score a 17.5, which will qualify him to attend Marquette University on a basketball scholarship.

In 1994, Russ Gough of Pepperdine University, along with several other college professors, took a hard look at the NCAA admissions standards. In an article for the *Sporting News*, Gough concluded that the eligibility rules are harmful to student athletes. Gough and the others found little evidence that the standards excluded only students who would not have succeeded in college. In fact, says Gough, "several studies . . . suggest many, if not most, of these casualties [excluded students] might well succeed." Gough maintains that standardized tests such as the SAT and ACT are the wrong basis for deciding eligibility for athletes. Gough, along with some members of the Black Coaches Association, maintains that standardized test scores indicate a test taker's family income more than his or her potential as a college student. Determining eligibility solely by test scores automatically eliminates many students, often minorities, who come from low-income neighborhoods.

Some observers believe, however, that higher standards are good for low-income minority students, many of whom may never have been challenged to do their best before. Arthur Padilla and LeRoy T. Walker, writing in the *Chronicle of Higher Education*, note that "evidence suggests that [Proposition 48] has had beneficial results." They note that football and basketball players actually did better in school after the rule was put into effect. They suggest that lowering standards sends a message to students that they are not expected to do well in high school or college.

Joe Paterno, head football coach at Penn State, agrees. He sees that high school students who want to play college sports have responded to the challenge to be better students. By lowering standards, Paterno believes, "we would have been saying that we don't have enough confidence" in their ability to achieve in school.

Others feel that the standards are still not strict enough. Burton F. Brody, a professor at the University of Denver College of Law, stated in a 1994 article in the *Sporting News*: "The NCAA should enact a rule that athletic grants-in-aid [scholarships] can be given only to students who are competitively admissible to the institution." In other words, Brody believes that only individuals who are otherwise qualified to be students at a particular school should be allowed to play sports at that school.

Do colleges put winning first?

The ideal of college athletes as students who just happen to play a sport does not always mix well with the way college athletic programs are run today. While the ideal may hold true for some smaller sports, football and basketball programs in particular are costly, professionally run organizations. Their goals may have little to do with scholarship. Athletic directors and coaches want to win games because that brings in more fans and more money. Isiah Thomas, who played basketball for Indiana University before making it in the NBA, says:

> When you go to college, you're not a student-athlete, but an athlete-student. Your main purpose is not to be an Einstein but a ballplayer, to generate some money, put people in the stands.

Like professional sports, college sports are big business. Dick DeVenzio is a former college basketball player and coach who now runs basketball camps and gives motivational speeches. DeVenzio says, "What's the reason universities have big-time sports? For the diversity? Because they like the smell of sweat? How about for the money?"

In 1994, the NCAA signed a $1.75 billion contract giving CBS the right to televise the Division I men's basketball tournament for the next eight years. CBS would not be willing to pay that kind of money if people were not watching, and fans like to watch winners. College president John Slaughter says, "Winning is the thing that ensures the income. Football and basketball have to make money, and they have to win to make money, and that's how the cycle becomes so vicious." Coaches agree that winning at all costs is sometimes the message they receive. One successful football coach says, "I'll be fired for losing before I'm fired for cheating."

Pay for college athletes

Many supporters of college sports point out that successful sports teams help their schools in other ways, by increasing the college's national prestige, for instance, and increasing donations from alumni and other supporters. Steve Bilsky, the athletic director of the University of Pennsylvania (Penn), reports that the school is gaining new students because of Penn's athletic successes. According to Tim Layden in *Sports Illustrated*:

> A member of the Penn admissions staff sought out Bilsky last fall and told him that a prospective Penn student—not an athlete—from Nebraska had just been interviewed. "The kid told our admissions officer that he had never heard of Penn until Penn played Nebraska in the NCAA basketball tournament," says Bilsky. A smile creases Bilsky's

face. "Television," he says. "You can't overstate its importance."

College athletes who draw fans, money, and prestige to their schools sometimes feel they should get something more than a chance to study and play their sport. Some athletes and others say that college athletes are essentially professionals and should be paid.

In 1994, the *Miami Herald* reported that several University of Miami football players had been accepting money from a group of boosters that included former team members and rap singer Luther Campbell of 2 Live Crew. The athletes knew the practice was against NCAA rules, but felt the rules were wrong. Tight end Randy Bethel said, "They want us to be like regular students. But regular students don't generate revenue like we do. I don't remember the last time 70,000 people packed into the Orange Bowl [stadium] to watch a chemistry experiment."

The Miami athletes and others like them feel that their value to the school—putting people in

Thousands of fans fill a stadium to watch a college football game. Some think college athletes should be paid because they generate money for their schools.

the stands—deserves some payment. Dick DeVenzio agrees that college football and basketball players should be paid some of the money they make for schools. By not paying players, he believes, schools take advantage of their athletic skills for the school's financial gain. DeVenzio and others, like sportswriters John Feinstein and John Rooney, have proposed that college athletes be paid, but that the money should be available only after a player graduates. Players who leave college early for a professional contract would forfeit their share—but they probably would not need it, anyway. As Feinstein says, the money would be there for "football and basketball players who do not become millionaires" when they leave college. The restriction of the money to those who actually graduate "would give a lot of mid-level athletes an incentive to stick with their classes."

The value of education

Others, such as *Sports Illustrated*'s Alexander Wolff, believe that college athletes are already being paid very well with a college education worth thousands of dollars. Dana Brooks, dean of the School of Physical Education at West Virginia University, believes that a college degree is far more valuable than any amount of cash:

> My position has been, and will forever be, that student athletes *are* compensated adequately by that scholarship, by that room and board. Let's remember that they're on campus to be students first and student-athletes second. They get quality coaching, trips to distant cities and access to a network of people with connections. Those athletes who don't go to the pros tend to get jobs in their own communities after college. If you cost all that out, it's worth quite a bit.

College presidents and NCAA officials in general oppose any talk of paying athletes. The expense of such payment is an issue for them, but so is their belief in the tradition of amateur athletics. Joseph Crowley, president of the University of Nevada and a former NCAA president, speaks for many when he says, "The day our members [NCAA schools] decide it's time to pay players will be the day my institution stops playing."

Outlook for the future

The NCAA, as the governing body for college sports, has taken steps to deal with some of the issues raised here. In 1993 it created a certification system for colleges to use to review their own programs. Each institution is to conduct an internal analysis, which will then be reviewed by independent sports officials. Each college must examine how its athletic programs are run and how well it follows NCAA rules, how its athletes are performing as college students, how the athletic departments are managing their money, and how well they are providing equal opportunity for all athletes, male and female.

Supporters of this approach believe that it will help college sports and encourage reform by forcing the schools "to engage in periodic soul-searching." Others are skeptical. Gary R. Roberts of Tulane University says, "It's adding an incredible amount of bureaucratic paperwork and rigmarole to a system where we're trying to cut costs." He does, however, believe that the review will force some institutions "to clean up their act a little bit." John Weisart, a sports law expert from Duke University, wonders "whether colleges themselves really want to reform, and whether the American public wants college sports to reform." In the long run, Americans will have to decide whether and how sports and schooling can coexist on college campuses.

3

Is Sexism a Problem in Sports?

FOR NEARLY TWO HUNDRED years, American women and sports had little to do with one another. While men have competed in games, contests, and teams since the beginning of our country and have been members of paid professional teams for more than a hundred years, women have been on the sidelines until recently. In the 1990s, women's sports are gaining a new visibility. The recent popularity of women's college basketball, women's Olympic events, and new women's professional baseball and basketball teams are signs that women are taking a bigger role in sports in America. Still, sports remain heavily dominated by men. Why? Some people believe that it is simply a matter of the differing physical abilities of men and women. Others believe that there is active discrimination against women in sports.

Discrimination forbidden by law

A new era in women's sports began in 1972, when Congress passed a law forbidding discrimination against women in schools and colleges that

(Opposite page) University of Georgia guard Saudia Roundtree drives the ball around University of Tennessee guard Latina Davis during a 1995 playoff game. While women's sports are gaining in popularity, college and professional sports still remain heavily dominated by men.

35

received federal funds. Under the law's requirements, if a school's enrollment was 50 percent male and 50 percent female, then 50 percent of its athletes would be male and 50 percent female. The same amount of money would be available to men's and women's teams for scholarships, equipment, coaching, travel, and so on. The law, known as Title IX of the Education Amendments Act, states that any organization that receives federal funds (including most high schools and colleges) may not discriminate according to sex. Schools that receive government money are required to provide the same opportunities for female students that they do for male students. Today, more than twenty years after its passage, public high schools and colleges are still a long way from providing equality for male and female athletes.

Progress stalls

From 1972 to 1978, girls' participation in high school and college sports increased dramatically. Since then, the numbers have remained fairly constant. Kathryn Reith of the Women's Sports Foundation looks at these figures and asks, "Has progress stalled? I would argue forcefully that it has. . . . Within the first six years of Title IX, we came a long way, but not far enough."

The amount of money available to men's and women's teams has leveled out, as well. Before Title IX, women's sports claimed a tiny piece of the athletics budget at most colleges. One large midwestern university spent $1,300 on men's athletics for every dollar spent on women's sports. Another university spent a total of $1,900 for women's sports, but $2 million for men's. By 1990, the schools with the biggest athletic programs, including football, spent 82 percent of their budget on men's programs and 18 percent

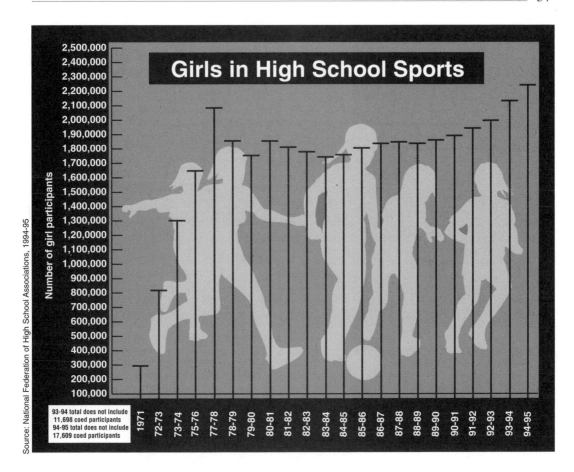

Girls in High School Sports

Number of girl participants

2,500,000
2,400,000
2,300,000
2,200,000
2,100,000
2,000,000
1,90,0000
1,800,000
1,700,000
1,600,000
1,500,000
1,400,000
1,300,000
1,20,0000
1,100,000
1,000,000
900,000
800,000
700,000
600,000
500,000
400,000
300,000
200,000
100,000

1971 72-73 73-74 75-76 77-78 78-79 79-80 80-81 81-82 82-83 83-84 84-85 85-86 86-87 87-88 88-89 89-90 90-91 91-92 92-93 93-94 94-95

93-94 total does not include
11,698 coed participants
94-95 total does not include
17,609 coed participants

Source: National Federation of High School Associations, 1994-95

on women's. Expenditures in smaller schools without football teams averaged 54 percent men's to 46 percent women's. Kathryn Reith believes that these figures show that "We're sort of stuck at the level of discrimination they [the schools] are comfortable with."

But Title IX remains the law. It has been around for nearly a quarter of a century. Why isn't there complete equality of men's and women's athletic programs? There are two main reasons.

First, the law was written in very general terms. Congress and the courts spent years clarifying exactly what the law meant and what it covered. There was an attempt to exempt certain sports (men's football and basketball) from the law, based on a 1984 Supreme Court ruling that said Title IX applied only to programs that receive direct government funds. Technically, most athletic departments get money from their schools and it is the school, not the department, that receives the federal money. In 1988, however, Congress passed the Civil Rights Restoration Act, which nullified the Supreme Court's earlier decision by declaring that sex discrimination was illegal in any department of a school which received federal money. So, sixteen years after its passage, Title IX finally was clarified.

Lack of enforcement

The second reason for the lack of equality is the failure of the government to enforce the law, or to investigate possible violations seriously. Arthur Bryant, executive director of Trial Lawyers for Public Justice, remarks:

> From my perspective, virtually every major educational institution . . . is in violation of Title IX. The problem is that the government is not enforcing the law. . . . Most universities recognize this. That's why they remain in violation.

Examples of inequities abound. The University of California, Santa Barbara, is one. UCSB has a men's basketball team and a women's basketball team. The women's team won the Big West Conference tournament in 1992 and 1993 and went on to win the first round of the NCAA tournament. The men's team has never won a Big West championship and hasn't made the NCAA playoffs for several years. Yet the women ride buses to most of their games, sometimes as long as twelve hours away. After the game, they ride the bus back home, getting what sleep they can. The men fly to their games and stay in comfortable hotels. The women's coach in 1993 was paid less than half the salary of the men's coach. The women's coach had one assistant; the men's coach had five.

This example is typical. Donna Lopiano, of the Women's Sports Foundation, testified before Congress in 1993 that "few if any institutions of higher education, or high schools for that matter, are complying with Title IX of the 1972 Education Amendments Act." Discriminatory traditional attitudes play a role. In the words of Ellen Vargyas, an attorney for the National Women's Law Center, there is "a firm conviction that women's sports are not as good, lucrative [profitable], or important as men's. Somehow, men's teams are more valuable, financially and cosmically."

But women athletes are beginning to demand their rights. Women are suing their schools for an equal share of the athletic budget. According to one estimate, there are at least sixty-five discrimination cases currently in court or being prepared for court. And women are winning. In the fall of 1995, according to *Women's Sports and Fitness* magazine, women had won thirty-one Title IX discrimination cases, and had lost none. In a noted recent case, Brown University was required to reinstate women's gymnastics and volleyball teams which had been cut from varsity status. Although Brown took the matter to a federal appeals court, the judge upheld the decision in favor of the women's teams, finding that the school, which is 51 percent female, did not offer equal athletic opportunities to women.

Not enough to go around?

Colleges offer various explanations for not providing equal funds to men's and women's sports. But for most, the key concern is not having enough money to go around. Because money is tight at schools everywhere, administrators say they will have to downgrade or eliminate some men's sports in order to upgrade women's sports.

But there may be ways to even out funding levels without hurting existing programs. For example, Donna Lopiano suggests that cuts in football could be made without harming football and without causing deep cuts to anyone else. She suggests limiting the number of players on football teams to 85, rather than the 125 to 150 that many of the larger schools have. The schools could then limit the number of football scholarships; fewer football players would get full scholarships, but the savings would be enough to fund three or four new women's sports, and meanwhile football and the other men's sports would remain intact. The NCAA has so far been reluctant to require these types of changes.

Should women run women's sports programs?

The effects of Title IX can be seen in other areas of women's sports, although not always with the intended outcome. Before Title IX, over 90 percent of all girls' and women's teams at high schools and colleges were coached by women. In 1992, according to a national survey conducted for the Women's Sports Foundation and the National Federation of State High School Associations, only 36 percent of girls' teams were coached by women.

After Title IX was passed and women's sports received more funding and gained in popularity, many new coaching positions opened up, with dramatically improved salaries. Most of those new positions were taken by male coaches, who had more experience than the women who were applying. What's more, most schools combined their men's and women's programs under the administration of the schools' athletic directors, who were almost exclusively male. When the ath-

A high school basketball coach rallies her team at half time. Women often find it difficult to secure coaching positions.

letic directors needed new coaches, they looked around at the people they already knew who were involved in athletics: again, almost all were men. Donna Lopiano says, "The athletic directors were primarily male, and their hiring network was primarily males. It was not intentional discrimination, but there was the assumption that men were better qualified."

Clarence Doninger, athletic director at Indiana University, says, "We would like to find more women coaches. But, frankly, the pool we draw from has a lot more men in it, some with more experience." Women, however, claim that athletic directors and college presidents hold women to a higher standard than they do men. Women become frustrated when they see coaching and administrative jobs going to men who have less experience but who are former professional athletes or who are friends of the athletic director. In 1988, Charlotte West, acting athletic director at Southern Illinois University, had thirty years of experience in sports administration at the college. But when it came time to select a permanent new director, the school selected Jim Hart, who had no administrative experience, but who had once been the quarterback for the St. Louis Cardinals. The college's president defended the selection of Hart by saying, "These jobs can be learned."

Connie Phorngren, of Boise State University, interviewed women coaches and asked them about their experiences in college athletics. Most of the women felt that they had second-class status in their athletic departments and that they were isolated from the male athletic director and male coaches. Many felt that they had to work harder than the male coaches to be accepted and respected. Phorngren concluded, "With a male coach, it's assumed they're capable until they prove they're not. With women, they have to prove they're capable. Women feel they can't make mistakes."

Do women's sports get fair treatment from the media?

Women athletes have also found that they must prove their sports events worthy of public, and thus media, interest in order to obtain media coverage. Supporters of women's sports believe that the media have ignored women's sports because the media are themselves predominantly male. In the words of Mariah Burton Nelson, former Stanford basketball player and author of *Are We Win-*

ning Yet? How Women Are Changing Sports and Sports Are Changing Women, "Information about women athletes is filtered through male writers, photographers, broadcasters, and publishers." Those same media professionals believe that the public is primarily interested in men's sports, and that their lopsided coverage only reflects what the public wants to see.

Between August 1972 and September 1973, NBC televised 366 hours of sports. One of those hours was about women's sports, less than 1 percent of the total coverage. During the same period, CBS devoted 10 of their 260 hours, or about 4 percent, of sports coverage to women's sports. More than twenty years later, a 1994 survey by the Amateur Athletic Foundation (AAF) showed that local television stations still devote only about 5 percent of their sports coverage to

A television reporter interviews heptathelete Jackie Joyner-Kersee after her victorious finish. Television networks devote only a small portion of their sports coverage to women's sports.

women's sports. The same survey counted sports stories in 4 newspapers and found that stories on men's sports outnumbered those on women's sports by 23 to 1.

During the 1990s, however, women's sports have started to win the attention of editors, writers, and programming directors. The popularity of women's basketball, especially during the NCAA tournament season, has been one major factor. In March 1995 the NCAA women's basketball championship game between the University of Connecticut and the University of Tennessee drew ten thousand spectators, and millions more watched on TV. The game, which was broadcast on CBS, drew more viewers than an NBA game on NBC and an NHL (National Hockey League) game on Fox at the same time.

University of Connecticut guard Jennifer Rizzotti charges toward the basket during the 1995 NCAA women's championship game. The televised game drew millions of viewers, demonstrating a growing interest in women's sports.

Such ratings victories have convinced some television executives that there is an audience for women's sports.

Dramatic increases in participation by girls and young women in school and organized youth sports over the past twenty-five years also translate to a larger viewing audience for women's sporting events. Fewer than three hundred thousand girls played on high school sports teams in 1971, compared with over two million today. About a third of all college athletes are women, compared to 9 percent in 1972, and more women than men choose individual sports such as swimming, bicycle riding, and aerobic dance. These numbers are likely to translate into added viewers. As Brooke Grabarek of *Financial World* says, "If they play, they are probably going to watch."

If women's sports were marketed and publicized as heavily as men's sports are, everyone involved in sports would benefit. Sports analyst Richard Lapchick, writing in the *Sporting News*, says, "By marketing women's sports, we can create yet another fan base of women who might enjoy the games enough that they begin to support men's sport as well. Let male fans see top-flight women's sports and they might become fans of what are new sports to them."

Can men and women compete on equal ground?

The growing number of girls and young women who are actively involved in sports has led to improved performance and a growing wish to compete and excel at the highest levels, which usually means with and against boys. In the 1993–1994 school year, 334 girls played on boys' football teams in high schools across the country; ten years before, there were only 13 girls on boys' teams. In baseball, girls' participation on boys' teams grew from 137 to 353 in the same ten years. In wrestling, there were 783 girls on boys' wrestling teams compared to none ten years before.

Not everyone agrees that this is necessarily good. One girls' softball coach thinks girls should concentrate on softball rather than baseball (with boys) because "There's a future for them in softball because of college scholarships." Others say that women's competing against men ultimately damages women's sports. In tennis, for example, where there is an active women's tour, a woman can be a star. Steffi Graf, the world's top-ranked woman tennis player, earned $8.5 million in

Victoria Roach smiles as she leaves the field after playing in a boys' Little League World Series game. As athletic performance improves, some girls seek to play on boys' teams.

1995. Top men players, such as Pete Sampras and Andre Agassi, would probably overpower Graf because of their size and strength, and Graf would be ranked much lower, with little opportunity to take home tournament money and endorsement extras.

Supporters of coed sports, however, argue that they are a good way for boys and girls to work together and to learn mutual respect. Girls who play with both boys and girls have a better body image during adolescence than girls who play only with girls, according to a 1985 study by the Women's Sports Foundation. Boys who play on the same teams with girls can learn to respect their abilities and to accept different styles of play. According to sports sociologist Don Sabo,

Steffi Graf, the world's top-ranked woman tennis player, earned $8.5 million in 1995. If she were to compete against men she would be ranked lower and would likely make far less money.

Some experts predict that women will be able to outrun men by the middle of the twenty-first century.

coed sports "can be very instructive for men." Sabo believes that in coed sports a boy or man can learn, for example, "to allow himself to cooperate rather than compete."

Women redefine their place in sports

In the past, men and women have been unable to compete on equal ground because of men's unquestioned athletic superiority. It is still unknown, however, how much of that superiority is due to men's physical size and strength and how much to more extensive training. Women swimmers and runners of the 1990s are competing at times that beat all male record holders of twenty years ago. Two researchers from the University of

California, Los Angeles, studied Olympic runners of the past century and compared rates of improvement between men and women. According to their study, women have improved at a faster rate than men, and if the trends of the past century continue, women could outrun men by the middle of the twenty-first century.

Whether or not women ever outrun or outswim or outplay men, it is certain that as we move into the twenty-first century more women than ever before will participate in sports. As women have redefined their place in society, they continue to redefine their place in the sports world, which is no longer exclusively male. Mariah Burton Nelson sums up what this new place has meant for women:

> They are getting pleasure out of sheer physical competence. They are taking physical risks and having fun in the process. Women athletes now have female stars to model themselves after, and those stars are gaining more fame and fortune than would have been thought possible twenty years ago. Sports participation has given millions of women new self-confidence and has taken them to where they never were before—onto what used to be male turf.

4

Race and Sports

A HALF CENTURY AGO the face of sports in America looked very different than it does today. Then, professional sports were completely white—no African-American athletes were allowed to play in the major leagues, and Hispanic and Native American athletes were tolerated only if their skin was light in color. In the 1990s, athletes of all races and many ethnic backgrounds can be found in professional sports. A corresponding racial and ethnic mix is not reflected in management and team leadership positions, however. Few teams have minority owners, managers, or coaches and team leadership positions are held mostly by white players.

Views differ as to the reasons for the dearth of minorities in management and leadership positions. One explanation is that change comes slowly and that minority representation has grown in the last few decades and will continue to do so in the future. However, racial stereotyping and discrimination are cited most often by those attempting to explain the absence of minorities in positions of power in the sports world today.

Segregation and discrimination

Only fifty years ago, racial discrimination was an accepted practice in American sports. Blacks

(Opposite page) Only within the past fifty years have athletes of different races competed together in professional sports. Though race relations within sports have improved, some feel that racism is still pervasive in professional sports.

were barred from participation in most professional sports. Jackie Robinson broke that barrier in major league baseball in 1947 when he stepped up to the plate as a member of the Brooklyn Dodgers.

But discrimination against black athletes did not end with Robinson's brave stand. The autobiographies of African-American baseball, basketball, and football players are full of sad tales of prejudice and exclusion. When teams went on the road during the 1950s and 1960s, black and white athletes frequently stayed in separate hotels and

As the first black man to play on a major league baseball team, Jackie Robinson paved the way for other minorities to enter professional sports.

ate in separate restaurants. Basketball great Bill Russell wrote in his 1979 autobiography, *Second Wind*, "As a rookie in 1957, I was the only black player on the Boston Celtics, and I was excluded from almost everything except practice and the games." Frank Robinson was the American League's MVP (Most Valuable Player) in 1966, but he was offered no endorsements and only one commercial and two speaking engagements. In contrast, Carl Yastrzemski, a white player who was the 1967 MVP, calculated that he received an extra $150,000 to $200,000 in endorsements and speaking engagements. Hank Aaron, the baseball great who broke Babe Ruth's career home run record in 1974, reported receiving death threats as he closed in on the record. Roger Maris, the white player who broke Ruth's single-season home run record in 1961, did not receive threats.

Changing statistics

Integrated rosters are the norm today. In 1994, according to Northeastern University's Center for the Study of Sport in Society, major league baseball was 19 percent black and 19 percent Hispanic; the NBA was 82 percent black, and the NFL was 69 percent black. Twenty-one of the world's forty highest-paid athletes in 1995, according to *Forbes* magazine, were African American, including all of the top six.

These numbers reflect a major change in America's attitude toward minorities in sports. In the 1950s and 1960s, minorities were accepted in sports—but just barely. They were expected to remain subordinate to white players. It took twelve years before every team in baseball was integrated, and seventeen years for professional football to attain that status. Black players rarely made top salaries in the early years. Today, sports are seen as a place where the races compete on an

Racial Composition of Players

	National Basketball Association NBA	National Football League NFL	Major League Baseball MLB
	1993-94	**1993**	**1994**
White	21%	35%	64%
Black	79%	65%	18%
Latino	0%	0%	18%
	1994-95	**1994**	**1995**
White	18%	31%	62%
Black	82%	68%	19%
Latino	0%	0%	19%

equal basis. Black players dominate some sports and make as much as or more than white players.

Minorities in management

This change in attitude has not yet fully translated to more minorities in management and leadership positions. Despite the large number of black football players, the NFL had no black head coaches until 1989, when Art Shell was hired to head the Los Angeles Raiders. During the 1970s and 1980s, a few blacks had brief stints as managers in baseball: Frank Robinson for the Indians, the Giants, and the Orioles, Maury Wills for the Mariners, and Larry Doby for the White Sox. But the 1990s mark the first time in baseball's history that several minority managers have been working at the same time, and successfully. Cito Gaston took over as manager of the Toronto Bluejays in 1989, leading the team to a division championship that year, American League pennants in 1991, 1992, and 1993, and World Series championships in 1992 and 1993. In 1993 Dusty Baker became the manager of the San Francisco Giants, leading the team to 103 wins and being named manager of the year. Don Baylor was chosen to manage the new Colorado Rockies that same year, and he took manager of the year honors in 1995. The NBA has had black coaches consistently since the Boston Celtics hired Bill Russell in 1966, and in the 1990s maintains the largest percentage of minority head coaches of any sport.

Colorado Rockies baseball team manager Don Baylor is one of a small group of minorities who has risen to professional sports management.

Top management in all sports, however, is still predominately white and male. Counting team presidents, vice presidents, general managers, chief executive officers (CEOs), and chairmen of the board—the positions that decide the major financial issues in all sports—the NBA has the highest number, with twenty-seven minority managers and owners (about 15 percent). The NFL has seven people of color in management, and baseball has ten (about 5 percent of top management in both cases).

Racial Composition of Head Coaches and Managers

	National Basketball Association NBA	National Football League NFL	Major League Baseball MLB
1993-94			
	1993		
		1994	
White	81% (22)	89% (25)	79% (22)
Black	19% (5)	7% (2)	14% (4)
Latino	(0)	<4% (1)	7% (2)
1994-95*	**1994**	**1995**	
White	81% (22)	93% (28)	82% (23)
Black	19% (5)	7% (2)	11% (3)
Latino	(0)	(0)	7% (2)

*The 1994-95 NBA figures do not include coaches named for Toronto and Vancouver for the 1995-96 season

Source: Northeastern University's Center for the Study of Sport in Society, 1995.

Historically, managers have been former players, often those who have held leadership positions on their teams, including what are known in some sports as "thinking positions" or "controlling positions." In football, the quarterback calls the plays and runs the offense. In baseball, the pitcher and the catcher decide how to play each batter, and they control the pace of the game.

These positions are still held mostly by whites. In 1990, 93 percent of NFL quarterbacks were white, while 88 percent of running backs and 96 percent of cornerbacks were black. In baseball, 87 percent of pitchers and 84 percent of catchers in the 1989 season were white, while 60 percent of outfielders were black or Hispanic. The positions held mostly by black players (running backs, outfielders) are positions which require players to react to the action on the field; they

Positions in the NFL by Race

OFFENSE	% of White Players 1994	% of Black Players 1994	DEFENSE	% of White Players 1994	% of Black Players 1994
Quarterback	91	9	Cornerback	1	99
Running Back	9	91	Safety	15	85
Wide Receiver	9	91	Linebacker	25	74
Center	80	19	Defensive End	25	73
Guard	54	43	Defensive Tackle	26	67
Tight End	38	60	Nose Tackle	43	57
Tackle	44	55			

Positions in Major League Baseball by Race

POSITION	% of White Players 1995	% of Black Players 1995	% of Latino Players 1995
Pitcher	75	8	17
Catcher	79	2	19
1st Base	65	24	11
2nd Base	51	21	28
3rd Base	66	13	21
Short Stop	40	13	47
Outfield	30	55	15

Source: Northeastern University's Center for the Study of Sport in Society, 1995.

don't determine it. Players who are not seen as being in charge on the field may be overlooked when it comes time to hire new coaches.

When it is time to hire a new manager or coach, owners and general managers tend to hire people they know and have worked with before, people they are comfortable with, and people they have seen taking leadership positions in the past. Over the years blacks, Hispanics, and whites in sports have tended to maintain some separation from one another, both socially and in the positions they play in the game. Thus, Jeffrey Benedict of the Center for the Study of Sport in Society describes the process: "it's who you know, who your friends are, and a lot of times, that small network is white people, and so minorities don't always get a fair shake from the start."

One reason that teams sometimes cite for their failure to hire minority managers and coaches is that the minority candidates don't have enough experience in leadership and management. Yet there is a long list of inexperienced white former players who have been hired as head coaches or managers. In many cases, they are former pitchers, catchers, or quarterbacks, all of which are key leadership positions on the field. For example, Frank Robinson spent twenty-one years in the major leagues, winning the MVP award in 1967, and spent several years managing in Puerto Rico but he was turned down for a managing job for the New York Yankees on the basis of lack of experience. Yet Robinson watched the Yankees hire Dick Howser and Lou Piniella, white former players with no managing experience at all. Robinson considers the "lack of experience" argument to be an excuse. He says, "One of the biggest cop-outs ballclubs use when they refuse to hire a black as a manager is, 'You don't have the experience.'"

Ingrained racial stereotypes

The question remains why minorities are not in those leadership positions where they can acquire experience. Some people think that although outright racism in sports has declined, racial stereotypes still exist. Racial stereotypes are beliefs that people act in certain ways because of their race. A 1991 *USA Today* poll found that both black and white people agreed that "white athletes are leaders and thinkers; blacks excel physically." According to Jim Myers in *USA Today*, " When asked to rate athletes on five skills, black and white respondents rate white athletes highest for 'leadership,' followed by 'thinking,' 'instincts,' 'strength,' and 'speed.' The skills of black athletes are rated in the exact opposite order."

Such stereotyping leads to common expectations: "white men can't jump," for example. White players are often said to succeed not because of natural ability but because they work harder at it and use their superior thinking skills.

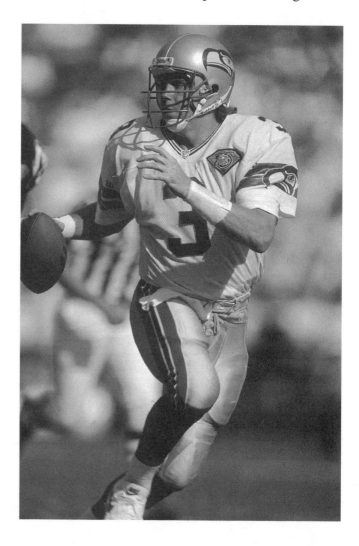

While blacks made up 68 percent of all NFL football players in 1994, 91 percent of NFL quarterbacks were white.

This attitude naturally causes resentment in black players who work just as hard. Isiah Thomas expressed his exasperation about this view of life in the NBA:

> When [Larry] Bird makes a great play, it's due to his thinking and work habits. It's all planned out for him. It's not the case for blacks. All we do is run and jump. We never practice or give a thought to how we play. It's like I came dribbling out of my mother's womb.

Richard Lapchick of the Center for the Study of Sport in Society believes that many coaches see black athletes in terms of stereotypes, just as the *USA Today* survey showed that many Americans do. Those who accept those stereotypes, says Lapchick, "may believe that blacks are less motivated, less disciplined, less intelligent, and more physically gifted." The coach who does believe the stereotypes acts on them and his expectations for his players are formed by them. According to college basketball coach John Thompson, one of the most outspoken members of the Black Coaches Association:

> In basketball it's been a self-fulfilling prophecy. White men run the game. A white coach recruits a good black player. He knows the kid's got talent, but he also knows that because he's black he's undisciplined. So he doesn't try to give the player any discipline. He puts him in the free-lance, one-on-one, hot dog role, and turns to the little white guard for discipline. Other black kids see this and they think this is how they are expected to play, and so the image is perpetuated.

Racism comes to light

One sensationalized 1987 incident brought the issue of racism in professional sports to light. In a network interview commemorating the fortieth anniversary of Jackie Robinson's entry into major league baseball, Dodger vice president for player

The stereotype that blacks succeed because of superior natural physical ability and whites achieve because of hard work and superior thinking skills still exists in sports.

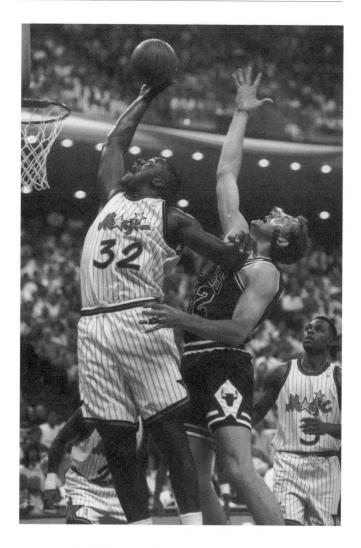

personnel Al Campanis was asked why there were no black managers, general managers, or owners in baseball, and if there was still prejudice against blacks in baseball. Campanis replied, "No, I don't believe it's prejudice. I truly believe they may not have some of the necessities to be, let's say, a field manager or perhaps a general manager." By "necessities" Campanis apparently meant intelligence, ambition, and leadership skills.

Campanis repeated other stereotypes in the course of his interview, saying that blacks were strong and fast, but did not have what it took to become leaders in baseball. Widespread outraged reaction was immediate, and Campanis was fired within days of his remarks, but many people felt and still feel that he was expressing an opinion shared by many in sports, as well as in the general public. The stereotypes may not even be conscious racism. Phillip Hoose, author of *Necessities: Racial Barriers in American Sports*, called Campanis's remarks "an intact record of the semiconscious values of those who control major sports in America."

The positive result of Campanis's remarks was that the American sports world could not avoid or dismiss the evidence that racism in sports remains a problem. Richard Lapchick has made a career of studying the relationship between race and sports. He says that Americans need to look at race and sports in the broader context of race and society. Lapchick is encouraged by recent trends, but points out that "sport free of racism can only exist in a society free of racism." He sees acceptance of minorities in all aspects of sports as one way to encourage acceptance of minorities in other aspects of society. Lapchick looks at sports in America and muses, "Using sport to break down racial and ethnic barriers seems so straightforward. How to get it done and sustain it is, of course, an issue for our collective lifetime."

5

Are Drugs a Problem in Sports?

DRUG USE AND ABUSE occurs in the sports world much as it does in the general population. Some athletes use drugs only under medical supervision and for a specific ailment or temporary condition. However, many athletes use drugs for more controversial reasons. Certain drugs can enhance an athlete's performance; others can temporarily provide thrills, escape from problems, or relief from stress.

Performance-enhancing drugs, especially those classified as steroids, have been banned from many sports. But despite bans, they are used by athletes in nearly every sport. "You show me a sport where increased power, endurance, or speed can possibly benefit the athlete, and I'll show you a sport where [steroid] use exists," says Dr. Robert Voy, chief medical officer of the U.S. Olympic Committee (USOC) during the 1984 Olympics.

Drug use by athletes prompts many of the same concerns as drug use by nonathletes, and for many of the same reasons. Both steroids and recreational drugs can cause problems for those

(Opposite page) While most athletes endure strenuous workouts to build their strength, some rely on performance-enhancing drugs to get an edge on the competition.

65

who use them. Addiction is a common risk with recreational drug use. Drug addiction has destroyed many lives, many careers, and many families. Steroids have been shown to damage the liver, heart, and arteries and to alter reproductive system function. They can also cause mood swings and lead to aggressive behavior.

The sporting world also wrestles with drug use issues that are unique to athletic competition. Probably the most intriguing debate surrounds the fairness of the competition. Do performance-enhancing drugs give an unfair advantage to those who use them? Views on this question are divided. Some believe that such drugs are just another means of preparation and training, while others say they destroy the spirit of the contest as a true test of one individual's skill against another's.

Whether or not drugs affect fair competition, drug tests are now a routine procedure at certain sporting events. First-, second-, and third-place finishers in Olympic events, for example, are routinely tested for a long list of unapproved drugs. A positive test is grounds for disqualification. Disqualification for drug use can be devastating to an athlete's career. For this reason, testing is carefully monitored to prevent errors. But errors do occur, and the possibility of false positives or false negatives leads some people to question the value of drug testing. Opposition to drug testing has also been voiced by those who believe that an athlete should be free to make private decisions about his or her training and preparation—including the use of drugs that might improve athletic performance.

Enhancing performance with drugs

Use of performance-enhancing substances is not new in the history of sport. In the ancient Olympic Games, athletes ate certain mushrooms

Olympic swimmers leap to the start of a 100-meter freestyle race. The top three finishers must undergo drug testing before they are declared Olympic champions.

to improve their performances. Roman gladiators and medieval knights may have used stimulants to help them when they were too tired or hurt to go on otherwise. In 1904 an Olympic marathoner, hoping to increase his speed and endurance, nearly died from taking a concoction of egg whites and a stimulant called strychnine, a substance used today primarily as a rat poison. During the 1940s a class of drugs called amphetamines (stimulants also known as "speed" or "pep pills") became very popular, especially among long-distance runners and cyclists.

Today, the most prevalent performance-enhancing drugs are a type known as anabolic-

The Wizard of Id. Reprinted by permission of Johnny Hart and Creators Syndicate, Inc.

androgenic steroids (AAS). These are substances derived from human hormones that can increase a person's strength and power. Although they are properly called by their full name, they are often referred to as anabolic steroids, or just steroids. "Anabolic" refers to the muscle-building effects of these hormones. "Androgenic" means "male-producing" and refers to the masculinizing effects of the hormones.

These steroids are a laboratory-made version of the natural male hormone testosterone. It is the normal production of testosterone in the teenage male's body that causes him to develop a deep voice, facial hair, and bigger muscles. Artificial male hormones, or anabolic-androgenic steroids, produce the same effects. Athletes take them to encourage muscle growth, because larger muscles generally mean greater strength.

An instant success

Anabolic-androgenic steroids first became part of the American sports scene in the late 1950s. An American doctor, John B. Ziegler, went to Moscow as part of the medical staff for the 1956 World Games. While there, he confirmed rumors that the Soviets were experimenting with hormones to help their athletes improve performance. He found that the Soviets were giving their athletes straight artificial testosterone. Dr. Ziegler returned to the United States and set about looking for a way to give American athletes the same advantage the Soviet athletes sought. Dr. Ziegler and a pharmaceutical company together created Dianabol, also known as D-bol.

Dianabol was an instant success. Athletes found that it could indeed help them develop bigger muscles more quickly, and by the 1970s, athletes worldwide were using steroids. Shortly before the 1976 Olympics, however, the International Olympic Committee (IOC) and the USOC officially banned the use of steroids in competition. Their position then, as now, was that steroids created unfair competition by enhancing an athlete's performance by unnatural means. By that time, however, steroids were a part of the training program of many athletes, and their benefits seemed irresistible.

Canadian sprinter Ben Johnson is among those athletes who turned to steroids as part of his training. At the 1988 Olympics in Seoul, Korea, Johnson ran the 100-meter dash in world record time: 9.79 seconds. He was stripped of his gold medal, however, and his time was removed from the record books when he tested positive for steroid use after the race.

The dangerous lure of steroids

Johnson is hardly alone in the group of world-class athletes who have used steroids. After the Seoul Olympics, an anonymous Soviet coach told the *New York Times* that he thought as many as 90 percent of Olympic athletes used drugs. "It is . . . widely acknowledged that Johnson is distinguishable from many of his competitors not because he *used* steroids but because he was *caught*," writes Norman C. Fost, director of a medical ethics program at the University of Wisconsin.

The lure of steroids is strong despite widespread knowledge that large amounts or long-

Canadian sprinter Ben Johnson won the 100-meter dash at the 1988 Olympics in world-record time. He was stripped of his gold medal, however, when he tested positive for steroid use after the race.

term use can be harmful, even fatal. Side effects include premature balding, acne, and aggressive behavior. In women as well as men, steroids deepen the voice and encourage growth of facial hair.

Steroids can also lead to more serious health problems. They have been linked to a condition called peliosis hepatitis, in which liver tissue breaks down into blood-filled cysts. Cysts that grow quite large may rupture and bleed. Despite surgical efforts to save his life, one twenty-seven-year-old British bodybuilder bled to death after a blood cyst in his liver ruptured. Studies also show that steroids damage the heart and the circulatory system. Long-term use can cause hardening of the arteries, which in turn can result in damage to the heart, brain, and kidneys.

There are numerous examples of seemingly healthy young athletes developing life-threatening conditions—and in some cases dying from them—after continued use of steroids. Former bodybuilder Glenn Mauer, a devoted steroid user, suffered a stroke in 1983 at the age of thirty-three. One month later he had to undergo a quadruple heart bypass operation. Nine-time American powerlifting champion Larry Pacifico also underwent a quadruple bypass operation at age thirty-five due to a condition brought on by steroid use. Steven Vallie, a former high school football star and bodybuilder from New Haven, Connecticut, died of heart failure in 1989 at the age of twenty-one. An autopsy revealed that he had an enlarged and scarred heart, probably caused by extensive steroid use.

Pressures to use drugs

Athletes who would rather not use steroids, whether out of concern for personal health, fair competition, or simply observing the rules, feel pressure nonetheless to include them in their training regimen. As American shot-putter Augie Wolf says, "The pressure to take drugs is enormous. An athlete asks himself, 'Do I take drugs and win medals, or do I play fair and finish last?'"

American weight lifter Ken Patera was faced with this dilemma after losing the 1971 World Championships to Russian opponent Vasily Alexyev. Patera attributed his loss to steroid use by Alexyev. Stung by the loss, Patera vowed to even the next contest, at the 1972 Olympics in Munich. "Last year the only difference between me and him was I couldn't afford his drug bill," said Patera. "Now I can. When I hit Munich I'll weigh in at about 340, or maybe 350. Then we'll see which are better, his steroids or mine."

Steroids by themselves do not create large muscles. The athlete must still train and build up the muscles, so many athletes do not regard steroid taking as unfair in itself. They see steroids as no different from eating a well-balanced diet and going to the gym regularly. They say that since steroids are based on a natural human substance, there is no more wrong in taking them than there is in taking vitamin supplements. Norman Fost expresses this view when he asks: "What moral principle is involved in allowing runners to ingest some natural substances, such as vitamins or Gatorade, but not others, such as steroids?"

Should drug testing be required in sports?

Despite differences of opinion about steroid use, most international athletic competitions have banned them and test athletes for their presence. Some professional sports as well as college and high school sports also test athletes for illegal drugs, primarily heroin and cocaine. The reasons for the testing are varied, but generally testing is intended to protect athletes from harmful substances, to maintain fair competition, and to protect the sports themselves, both from bad publicity over stigmatized practices and from becoming events in which winning is acknowledged to be more important than sportsmanship. The teams and organizations hope that the possibility of being caught and disgraced will discourage drug use among athletes.

In addition to testing the first three finishers, some Olympic testing is done randomly: Before an event, three or four athletes are selected at random, and they must be tested after the event or be

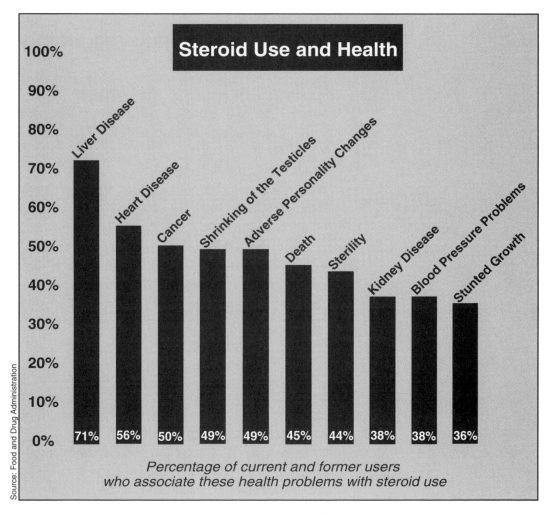

Steroid Use and Health

Liver Disease 71%
Heart Disease 56%
Cancer 50%
Shrinking of the Testicles 49%
Adverse Personality Changes 49%
Death 45%
Sterility 44%
Kidney Disease 38%
Blood Pressure Problems 38%
Stunted Growth 36%

Percentage of current and former users who associate these health problems with steroid use

Source: Food and Drug Administration

disqualified. Testing consists of providing a urine sample. To reduce the possibility of cheating, an official observer watches as the athlete urinates into a container that has two sections. Each section is sealed by the athlete, also in the presence of the observer, and the samples are assigned a code number, not the athlete's name. The samples are tested for the presence of certain specific drugs that are banned by the IOC. If an athlete's first sample is positive, the second sample is tested again, in the presence of additional qualified observers.

NCAA athletes must sign a drug-testing consent form. Athletes may be tested at random and at any time during the year if they are in Division I or II football or track and field. The NCAA also conducts drug tests during championship tournaments and football bowl games. Athletes who test positive lose a season of competition.

Support and opposition

The professional leagues allow drug testing of an athlete who has been convicted of a drug-related offense. In addition, the NBA has a policy of testing first-year players randomly. They may be tested as often as six times during their first season. After the first year, players are not randomly tested unless they behave in a way that causes suspicion that they are using illegal drugs. The NFL tests for steroid use, but the tests are scheduled, not random.

Some players strongly support drug testing, either because of personal objections to drug use or as a way to quiet rumors about who is or is not using drugs. Basketball star Charles Barkley of the Phoenix Suns is most concerned about recreational drug use. He believes strongly that "You can't use drugs. It's that simple." According to the *Sporting News*, Barkley's opposition to drug use is so strong that he would like to see random testing for everyone, with lengthy suspensions for athletes who test positive. First baseman Frank Thomas of the Chicago White Sox advocates testing for steroids. Thomas is a power hitter who gained thirty-five pounds between the 1994 and 1995 seasons. His weight gain prompted speculation that he was using steroids. Thomas has said publicly that he does not use steroids, but he believes testing would quiet all doubt.

> At least [testing] would get rid of the suspicions. I went in to see my doctor this winter, and he even

asked me, "Hey, are you on steroids?" It's a question people are going to ask, especially the big power hitters, unless something is done about it.

The players' associations for major league baseball, the NFL, the NBA, and the NHL have all strongly resisted any attempts to institute drug testing at that level. They regard it as a violation of the athletes' privacy rights. Professional athletes, the argument goes, are adults who are free to make decisions about the conduct of their own lives. Furthermore, they are protected, as are all citizens, under the Fourth Amendment to the U.S. Constitution, which prohibits "unreasonable

Chicago White Sox first baseman Frank Thomas favors mandatory testing for steroids. Thomas believes that testing would end suspicions and rumors about which professional athletes use them.

searches" of persons and property. Opponents to drug testing regard it as an unreasonable search. The players' associations were formed to speak for the players and to protect their rights; drug testing, in their view, is an invasion of privacy.

Other observers agree that drug testing on the basis of protecting athletes from harming themselves is unjustified and hypocritical. Sports themselves can be viewed as harmful to players. Serious injury and death from all forms of sport are not uncommon, but the sports are not consequently banned. Additionally, it is neither possible nor desirable to protect people from all the things they do that can harm themselves, and hundreds of thousands of people die every year because they choose harmful behaviors, such as smoking, heavy drinking, and unhealthy eating habits. Norman Fost expresses his disdain for the protection argument when he states, "If the health of athletes were truly the concern and the responsibility of the leaders of organized sports, then screening athletes for evidence of heavy smoking and drinking would seem a more justifiable or efficient program."

Drug tests okay in high schools

In 1995 the Supreme Court ruled that public junior high and high schools may constitutionally perform drug tests on their athletes. The schools need not suspect that a player is using drugs; they may test at any time. The case before the Court began in 1991 when a football player at an Oregon high school refused to take a urine test intended to screen athletes for use of amphetamines, marijuana, and cocaine. Officials of the Vernonia School District had instituted the testing policy because they felt they had a serious drug problem, largely among athletes. When James Acton refused to take the drug test, he was barred from

the school team. His parents sued the school district, arguing that Acton's Fourth Amendment rights had been violated by the policy.

In June 1995 the case reached the U.S. Supreme Court, which returned a majority opinion written by Justice Antonin Scalia stating that schools may conduct such drug tests. The decision emphasized the "importance of deterring drug use by all this nation's schoolchildren." Scalia referred to athletes as "role models" and also stated that drug use poses a particular physical danger to athletes, because drugs impair judgment, affect reaction time, and mask pain. Therefore, he said, it seems "self-evident" that such a drug problem would be "effectively addressed by making sure that athletes do not use drugs."

Scalia's decision maintained that privacy rights "are different in public schools than elsewhere"

A 1995 Supreme Court decision allows high schools to test student athletes for drugs.

and that "by choosing to 'go out for the team,' [students] voluntarily subject themselves to a degree of regulation even higher than that imposed on students generally." Justice Sandra Day O'Connor's dissenting opinion asserted that the type of drug testing that Vernonia was doing could be considered an unreasonable search within the meaning of the Fourth Amendment. She argued that testing only those reasonably suspected of drug use "would have gone a long way toward solving Vernonia's school drug problem while preserving the Fourth Amendment rights of James Acton and others like him."

What can drug tests accomplish?

Dave Kindred, writing about the case in the *Sporting News*, believes that random testing is unfair and unconstitutional. He argues that this sort of testing makes suspects out of all young athletes, who are forced to go along with the testing or give up their chance to play sports. He says, "It is ludicrous to believe that testing a few athletes—a minority at all schools—will prevent drug use by a majority of users." Kindred admits that not testing everyone may allow some drug users to get by. But that is better, he says, than "to tell millions of innocent children . . . that we think they could be guilty unless they prove to us, by handing over their urine, that they are innocent."

The Oregon case can help Americans clarify where they stand on the issue of drug use in sports. If drug use is such a serious problem that it must be stamped out, no matter what the cost to individual freedoms, then strict antidrug policies and testing will increase. If, on the other hand, drug use is regarded by most as a relatively minor problem in sports, policies will become less strict. Sports organizations and the American public need to examine the problem in more detail and determine whether all drug use goes against the ideals of sport, or whether, in fact, some drugs are simply training devices, like weight machines and specialized diets.

Do Young People Benefit from Organized Sports?

Twenty-five million children in the United States are involved in organized sports activities. Almost every community in the country has youth leagues for baseball, softball, basketball, soccer, and football, as well as swimming and gymnastics programs. Many adults believe that team sports are a vital part of growing up, that they teach valuable lessons for life, and that every child deserves the experience of sports participation. Others, however, believe that organized youth sports as they are run today overemphasize competition, create too much pressure on children, are unsafe, and should be changed in fundamental ways.

Benefits and pitfalls

According to the Institute for the Study of Youth Sports at Michigan State University, more than half of American boys and girls between the ages of six and eighteen "regularly take part in at least one organized sport." At their best, according to Kevin Cobb in *American Health* magazine, "sports help socialize children, promote mental

(Opposite page) Young athletes sprint down the field to score a goal for their team. While organized sports offer many benefits for children, parents and coaches sometimes place too much emphasis on winning.

and physical development, build self-esteem and strengthen family bonds." Critics of organized youth sports, however, feel that such programs are often not "at their best." They charge that sports leagues set up and run according to adult rules and expectations are concerned more with what adults need and want than with what children need and want. Rick Wolff, former baseball player and coach and author of *Good Sports*, believes that adults introduce children to the concepts of rules and of victory and defeat much sooner than children would arrive at those concepts themselves. This, he believes, destroys some of the fun of the game for children. When children are playing spontaneously, Wolff says, the important thing is the playfulness itself. When the concepts of rules and winning are introduced, the game becomes more serious. "After all," says Wolff, "there's no time to fantasize about one's play when one is being judged according to 'the rules of the game,' a game usually set up by—you guessed it—parents."

Is competition good for children?

Proponents of youth sports believe strongly that children who participate in sports activities are healthier and happier than children who do not. Sports psychologist Eric Margenau believes that the effect is long lasting, as such children also "grow up to become healthier adults." Margenau and Dr. Lyle Micheli, a sports physician specializing in children's sports medicine, both believe in the concept of healthy competition. This does not mean playing to win at all costs, but rather, as Micheli says, "to strive to win by playing as hard as they can within the boundaries of a set of rules."

Micheli also points out that competition among children did not begin with organized sports.

Children will naturally set up their own competitions and, like adults, they enjoy winning. But, he points out, "For kids, success in sports mostly means having fun. In fact, winning at all costs usually gets in the way of having fun; the game becomes too serious."

It is this winning-at-all-costs attitude that causes some critics to object to organized youth sports. Organized sports almost always involve rules that define the game in terms of competition. Alfie Kohn, author of *No Contest: The Case Against Competition*, argues that competition is "related to fear, possessiveness and selfishness." He says, "By definition, not everyone can win a contest. . . . Competition leads children to envy winners, to dismiss losers and to be suspicious of just about everyone."

Kohn believes that a competitive approach is all wrong for kids. He says, "There should be cooperation, bonding with others, appreciation for things

Kids naturally set up their own sports competition and get enjoyment out of it.

Softball players react jubilantly as one of their teammates scores a run. Although kids enjoy winning, the majority say having fun is more important to them.

well done, a sense of connectedness and shared experience." And, indeed, studies show that those are the goals that most children have when they get involved in sports. In the late 1980s, researchers from the University of California at Los Angeles interviewed nearly two thousand boys and girls who played on community sports teams in Southern California. According to the study, what children like best about sports are having the support and interest of their coach, learning and working with other kids on their team, having good experiences to share with their parents, enjoying a feeling of being good at a sport, feeling physically fit, and, last of all, winning.

Another part of the UCLA study asked the children why they joined a team in the first place. The children's top answers indicated that they wanted to have fun, to get better at their sport, and to enjoy a sport they were good at. Winning was not a major reason to play. Other studies over the years have supported these results. A major study in 1974 asked children about playing and winning. According to Rick Wolff, "Over 95 percent of the kids replied that they would rather simply have fun than worry about winning, and over 90 percent said they would prefer to be on a losing team if they were able actually to play in the games rather than be a benchwarmer on a winning team."

Pressure

Many people who are involved in youth sports confirm that adults—parents and coaches—are the ones who care most about winning. A Southern California mother whose husband coaches baseball says, "These are 6-, 7- and 8-year-olds, and [the parents] get so much more into it. They're yelling to do this, do that. The parents are living through their children."

Bill Geist agrees. A journalist, Little League coach, and author of *Little League Confidential: One Coach's Completely Unauthorized Tale of Survival*, Geist says:

> At the little local clinics, they always emphasize that It's All For Fun, Only a Game, Winning Is Not the Most Important Thing. So the kids might ask: why do the best players play the most important positions? Why does our coach jump up and down when we win, and call the other coach the A-word when we lose? And get mad when I strike out? Why do our parents scream so and call the umpire names? Everybody certainly acts as though winning were important.

Some parents admit that they care more about winning than their children do. A banker watching his seven-year-old son play baseball in Southern California says, "I'm more into it now than I was when I was playing. You live your life through your children." Psychologist Eric Margenau believes that parents put pressure on their children unintentionally. Pressure to play excellently and to win, according to Margenau, "says quite clearly to a child that performance is more important than participation, winning is more important than how you play the game, and, in fact, that there is nothing wrong with winning at all costs."

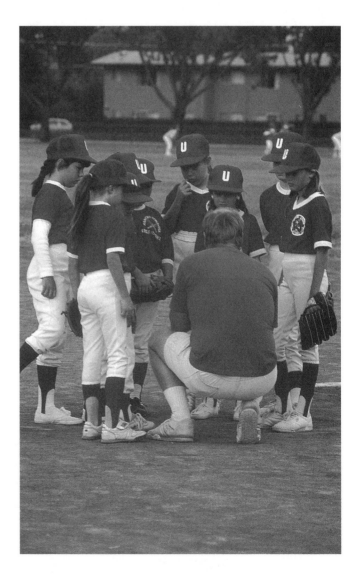

Young players huddle around their coach as he lays out the strategy for the rest of the game. Those involved with youth sports say coaches sometimes care more about winning than about making sure that all team members participate.

A 1990 poll conducted by NBC and *USA Today* found that 37 percent of children surveyed "wished that no parents would watch them play sports," and that 41 percent "said that they have awakened in the night worrying about an upcoming game." They worry because they feel under pressure to perform well. They worry that if they fail to perform they will be letting down their parents and their coach. Parents and coaches foster this idea when they focus on the results rather than on the play.

Rick Wolff believes there are ways children can play without adult pressures. He agrees with the recommendations of two psychologists who did a study of Little League play in the 1970s. In order to make sports more enjoyable for children, they suggested eliminating score books completely, letting children umpire or referee their

Untrained coaches may place harmful pressure on kids by promoting a win-at-all-costs attitude.

own games, letting each player play the same amount of time, being willing not to enforce a rule if it gets in the way of children's fun, and letting players select their own coaches. Wolff believes that the key to eliminating pressure and making sports more fun for children is to "let your top priority be the children's amusement and the sheer fun of playing the sport."

Should coaches be certified?

Wolff's suggestion that children select their own coaches grows out of concern that well-meaning but untrained coaches can contribute greatly to putting harmful pressure on young athletes. Recent efforts across the country would have all coaches of youth sports attend classes and earn certification. Supporters believe this is the best way to ensure that coaches understand both the physical and psychological needs of children. They believe that well-trained coaches understand healthy competition and pressure-free teaching and playing. There is no major opposition to this training effort, but it is a difficult goal to achieve, nevertheless, as youth coaches are almost all volunteers, mostly parents, who feel that they have far too much to do already.

Mike Pfahl, executive director of the National Youth Sports Coaches Association, notes, "We've got 100,000 members, but it's a drop in the bucket when you consider there are 3.5 million volunteer coaches in America." Most coaches are either unaware that training is available or hard pressed for time to participate. Most youth leagues do not require training because they find it hard enough to get volunteers to coach without adding extra requirements. And neither are parents insisting on trained coaches for their children. That amazes Pfahl:

> When parents take their 7-, 8-, or 9-year-old kids and put them into school, it's most important to them that they get a qualified teacher. But after school they're willing to release their children to volunteer coaches who don't have a clue what they're doing to these kids.

Helping coaches do a better job

Trained coaches are more likely to understand the emotional needs of their players and to emphasize the well-being of all players. This aspect is sometimes ignored when volunteer coaches care more about winning than about creating a positive experience for players.

In organized baseball or softball, for example, often the coach decides who plays, and where, and when. Whether or not that means equal play for everyone depends on the coach. Most leagues have rules that say that every player who shows up must be allowed to play at least half of the game in the field and have at least one at-bat. Some coaches, believing strongly in the spirit of the rule, will rotate all players, so that in each game, some players play the minimum and others play the entire game. Over the course of a season, everyone will play a more or less equal amount of time.

Other coaches will follow the rule to the letter, so that the worst player on the team will play exactly three innings of a seven-inning game in the field (probably as the right fielder, where fewest

Coaches who understand the emotional needs of their players can help create a positive experience for their team.

A young athlete throws a baseball with fierce determination. Sports for young people can foster self-confidence and promote mental and physical health.

balls are hit) and have one or two at-bats, depending on how well the rest of the team is hitting. One California mother watched her son's baseball team all season and said, "Of course, the best players get the most playing time, and the worst—who need the practice the most—get the least. How are they ever going to improve if they only get one chance per game to hit?"

Lyle Micheli believes that the advantages to having certified coaches will eventually outweigh the inconveniences of the training. He points out that Canada, Australia, and New Zealand are all now requiring certification of youth coaches, and he believes that Americans will follow suit. He sees it as a situation in which everyone wins:

> Our coaches will win: they'll be better trained and therefore more knowledgeable in sports technique,

health fitness principles, and injury prevention. Parents will win: they'll know that their children are being instructed by qualified personnel. And of course, the biggest winners will be our kids: they'll be better trained, less likely to be injured, and more qualified to participate in sports and health fitness activities throughout life.

Every year, about twelve million children are treated for sports injuries in emergency rooms and by family doctors. There is no way to know how many of those injuries occur in organized sports or in spontaneous play. The latter is harder to control than the former. But even in organized sports, safety issues sometimes become lost in the pursuit of winning.

Concern about safety

Most states and localities require safety equipment in youth sports. No child plays baseball in an organized league without wearing a batting helmet. More and more leagues are using breakaway bases, which reduce the incidence of torn ligaments and broken bones from sliding into base, or they bar sliding. Youth football players are required to wear protective padding and helmets, and soccer players wear shin guards. Parents and other volunteers help maintain the playing fields of youth sports leagues, assuring that they are free of glass and other debris that could cause injuries. All games are supervised by adults. All of these factors make organized youth sports much safer in many ways than those that young people play on their own.

Sometimes, however, safety equipment becomes controversial. Recently Little League commissioners in the Southern California city of Rancho Niguel voted not to allow use of the RIF (reduced injury factor), or safety, baseball because it would "violate baseball tradition." In fact, many Little Leagues in the country use the softer ball. According to one study, teams using the RIF ball had 73 percent fewer injuries than teams using the regular hardball. One parent objecting to the league's decision said she felt that the league was telling her that winning and "toughness" were more important than the safety of the children:

> I was told that if we proceeded to tournament play and were playing teams from Mission Viejo [a nearby town], and we were using the RIF ball and they weren't, we'd probably lose because they would be "tougher." So, "toughness"—and beating Mission Viejo—that's what really matters here. That was the message.

Broken arms, legs, and fingers, sprained ankles, and assorted cuts and bruises—typical

Most youth sports leagues require players to wear protective gear such as batting helmets for baseball players. Still, millions of children each year suffer from sports injuries that require medical care.

sports injuries—are nothing new. According to sports physician Lyle Micheli, however, the increase in organized sports for children has caused an increase in overuse injuries, the kinds of injuries that professional athletes are used to, caused by repetitive damage to the body's tissues and joints. Cautions Micheli:

> Overuse injuries were unknown in free play and sandlot sports. Hurt or sore athletes generally went home and didn't return to play until they felt better. But children in organized sports often overtrain and play when hurt. Kids may conceal sore elbows or aching knees because they don't want to look like sissies.

Micheli believes that most overuse injuries are the result of "uninformed coaches who make an 8-year-old heave a hardball over and over again, or swing a tennis racket again and again, too soon, or run and kick without warm-up exercises." Physical therapist and sports medicine specialist Mark Anderson agrees. He says, "Coaches need to be aware of the dangers of asking a player to try to do too much too early." Anderson believes that part of the problem is that professional athletes are admired for their ability to "play hurt," and children imitate the pros. But he points out that professional athletes are doing their job; children risk a lifetime of pain if they damage a growing body.

Lifetime fitness

Rather than a lifetime of pain, sports for children in the best circumstances promote a lifetime of fitness. In December 1993, the President's Council on Physical Fitness and Sports reported that even very young children in America are often unfit and exhibit at least one risk factor for heart disease: physical inactivity, obesity, high cholesterol, or high blood pressure. Organized

Ten Most Popular Boys' High School Sports

	Participants
1. Football	955,247
2. Basketball	540,269
3. Baseball	440,503
4. Track & Field (Outdoor)	430,807
5. Soccer	272,810
6. Wrestling	216,453
7. Cross Country	163,829
8. Golf	133,705
9. Tennis	132,735
10. Swimming and Diving	80,089

Ten Most Popular Girls' High School Sports

	Participants
1. Basketball	426,947
2. Track & Field (Outdoor)	360,223
3. Volleyball	340,176
4. Softball (Fast Pitch)	278,395
5. Soccer	191,350
6. Tennis	139,157
7. Cross Country	133,551
8. Swimming & Diving	106,467
9. Field Hockey	54,359
10. Softball (Slow Pitch)	35,691

Source: National Federation of High School Associations, 1994-95.

sports can fill the need for physical activity, as well as provide young people with skills, friendships, and fun. It is up to children and their parents to insist on the best, however: well-organized, well-coached, safe sports that are fun for kids. In the words of sports doctor Lyle Micheli, "That virtually guarantees a lifetime interest in sports and fitness."

Suggestions for Further Reading

Nathan I. Aaseng, *The Locker Room Mirror: How Sports Reflect Society*. New York: Walker & Co., 1993.

Madeleine Blais, *In These Girls, Hope Is a Muscle*. Boston: Atlantic Monthly Press, 1995.

Gary Funk, *A Balancing Act: Sports and Education*. Minneapolis: Lerner Publications, 1995.

Hoop Dreams, New Line Home Video, 1995 (film).

Evaleen Hu, *A Level Playing Field: Sports and Race*. Minneapolis: Lerner Publications, 1995.

Scott E. Lukas, *Steroids*. Hillside, NJ: Enslow Publishers, 1994.

Hank Nuwer, *Sports Scandals*. New York: Franklin Watts, 1994.

Rodney G. Peck, *Drugs and Sports*. New York: Rosen Publishing Group, 1992.

Joan Ryan, *Little Girls in Pretty Boxes: The Making and Breaking of Elite Gymnasts and Figure Skaters*. New York: Doubleday, 1995.

Alvin Silverstein, Virginia Silverstein, and Robert Silverstein, *Steroids: Big Muscles, Big Problems*. Hillside, NJ : Enslow Publishers, 1992.

Katherine S. Talmadge, *Drugs and Sports*. Frederick, MD: Twenty-First Century Books, 1991.

Ann E. Weiss, *Money Games: The Business of Sports*. Boston: Houghton Mifflin, 1993.

Rick Wolff, *Good Sports: A Concerned Parent's Guide to Little League and Other Competitive Youth Sports*. New York: Dell, 1993.

Works Consulted

Books

Susan K. Cahn, *Coming on Strong: Gender and Sexuality in Twentieth-Century Women's Sport*. New York: The Free Press, 1994.

William Dudley, ed., *Sports in America: Opposing Viewpoints*. San Diego: Greenhaven Press, 1994.

Jerry Gorman and Kirk Calhoun, with Skip Rozin, *The Name of the Game: The Business of Sports*. New York: John Wiley & Sons, 1994.

Dale Hoffman and Martin J. Greenberg, *Sport$biz: An Irreverent Look at Big Business in Pro Sports*. Champaign, IL: Leisure Press, 1989.

Phillip M. Hoose, *Necessities: Racial Barriers in American Sports*. New York: Random House, 1989.

Richard Lapchick, *Five Minutes to Midnight: Race and Sport in the 1990s*. Lanham, MD: Madison Books, 1991.

Eric A. Margenau, *Sports Without Pressure: A Guide for Parents and Coaches of Young Athletes*. New York: Gardner Press, 1990.

Mike Messerole, ed., *The 1995 Information Please Sports Almanac*. Boston: Houghton Mifflin, 1995.

Lyle J. Micheli, with Mark D. Jenkins, *Sportswise: An Essential Guide for Young Athletes, Parents, and Coaches*. Boston: Houghton Mifflin, 1990.

National Collegiate Athletic Association, *1995–96 NCAA Guide for the College-Bound Student Athlete.* Overland Park, KS: NCAA, 1995.

———, *1993–94 NCAA Annual Reports.* Overland Park, KS: NCAA, 1995.

Mariah Burton Nelson, *Are We Winning Yet? How Women Are Changing Sports and Sports Are Changing Women.* New York: Random House, 1991.

James Quirk and Rodney D. Fort, *Pay Dirt: The Business of Professional Team Sports.* Princeton, NJ: Princeton University Press, 1992.

Lee R. Schreiber, *The Parents' Guide to Kids' Sports.* Boston: Little, Brown, 1990.

Nathan J. Smith, Ronald E. Smith, and Frank L. Smoll, *Kidsports: A Survival Guide for Parents.* Reading, MA: Addison-Wesley, 1983.

Murray Sperber, *College Sports Inc.: The Athletic Department vs. the University.* New York: Henry Holt, 1990.

Robert Voy, with Kirk D. Deeter, *Drugs, Sport, and Politics.* Champaign, IL: Leisure Press, 1991.

Periodicals

Kelli Anderson, "No Room at the Top," *Sports Illustrated,* September 28, 1992.

Associated Press, "Dispute Warms Up over Olympic Jackets," *San Jose Mercury-News*, July 30, 1992.

Joseph Basralian, "Amateurs . . . at Best," *Financial World,* February 14, 1995.

Ron Berler, "America's Push for a Rich Career in Sports Can Be a Trial for Youngsters," *Salt Lake Tribune*, June 14, 1992.

Debra E. Blum and Douglas Lederman, "NCAA Votes to Retain Tougher Standards," *Chronicle of Higher Education*, January 20, 1995.

Don L. Boroughs with Robin M. Bennefield, "Playing the Money Game," *U.S. News & World Report*, May 15, 1995.

Ellis Cashmore, "Run of the Pill," *New Statesman & Society*, November 11, 1994.

Howard Eskin, "Barkley: Race a Team Priority," *Philadelphia Daily News*, October 30, 1991.

David Falkner, "The American Way," *The Sporting News*, February 13, 1995.

Russ Gough, "The Hard Facts on Propositions 48 and 16," *The Sporting News*, September 26, 1994.

Brooke Grabarek, "Ladies, Don't Touch That Dial," *Financial World*, February 14, 1995.

Michael Granberry, with Rodney Foo, "Playing Hardball: Little League Chapter Rejects Call for Safer Ball," *San Jose Mercury-News*, May 15, 1995.

David Guterson, "Moneyball!: On the Relentless Promotion of Pro Sports," *Harper's Magazine*, September 1994.

Jane O'C. Hamilton, "The Hoopla over Women's Hoops," *Business Week*, April 10, 1995.

Rich Hoffman, "What He Says All Adds Up," *Philadelphia Daily News*, October 31, 1995.

"Indecent Proposal," *Sports Illustrated*, July 17, 1995.

Jillian Kasky, "The Best Ticket Buys for Sports Fans Today," *Money*, October 1995.

Richard L. Kenyon, "Kids at Play," *Milwaukee Journal*, July 5, 1992.

Dave Kindred, "Constitutional Rights—and Wrongs," *The Sporting News*, July 10, 1995.

———, "For Love, Not Money," *The Sporting News*, December 5, 1994.

Jerry Kirshenbaum, "A Pain in the Masses," *Sports Illustrated*, December 19, 1994.

Michael Knisley, "*The Sporting News* 100 Most Powerful," *The Sporting News*, January 2, 1995.

Randall Lane, "A Very Green 1995," *Forbes*, December 18, 1995.

Richard Lapchick, "The Grades Are In," *The Sporting News*, September 18, 1995.

———, "Women's Basketball as a Hoop du Jour," *The Sporting News*, April 24, 1995.

Cathy Lawhon and Renee Tawa, "Are Child Athletes and Parents Playing the Same Game?" *Orange County Register*, May 17, 1992.

Tim Layden, "Winning Ways," *Sports Illustrated*, August 28, 1995.

Jody Meacham, "When Men Coach Women: A Mercury-News Special Report," *San Jose Mercury-News*, November 27, 1994.

Stuart Miller et al., "Playing with the Big Boys," *Women's Sports and Fitness*, April 1995.

Susan L. Morse, "Women and Sports," *CQ Researcher*, March 6, 1992.

Bob Nightengale, "Steroids in Baseball? Say It Ain't So, Bud," *The Sporting News*, July 24, 1995.

Andrew Osterland, "Field of Nightmares," *Financial World*, February 14, 1995.

Michael Ozanian, "Following the Money," *Financial World*, February 14, 1995.

Michael Ozanian and Stephen Taub, "Adam Smith Faces Off Against Karl Marx," *Financial World*, February 14, 1995.

Arthur Padilla and LeRoy T. Walker, "The Battle for Control of College Sports," *Chronicle of Higher Education*, December 14, 1994.

Shaun Powell, "Finding Reasonable Cause for a Drug Policy Tune-Up," *The Sporting News*, April 3, 1995.

Susan Ray, "NFL Fan Cost Index Up," *Amusement Business*, October 3, 1994.

"Readers: Just Leave the 'Stick Alone," *San Jose Mercury-News*, September 10, 1995.

Danny Robins, "A Question of Responsibility: Are There Academic Obligations to Athletes?" *Los Angeles Times*, April 12, 1992.

Ron Rosenbaum, "The Revolt of the Basketball Liberals," *Esquire*, June 1995.

Skip Rozin, "The Color of Money: Fashion Spurs Licensing Profits," *Sport*, February 1995.

————, "New Money and Old Games: The Hows and Why of Salary Escalation," *Sport*, November 1994.

———, "Scoring for Fun and Profit: How the Two-Point Conversion Converts to Dollars," *Sport*, January 1995.

Ron Scherer, "Women Athletes Ponder Goals; Among Them: Pro Sports, More Money, and More Media Attention," *Christian Science Monitor*, October 28, 1994.

Linda Tsai, "The Biggest Players in Sports for Today's Teams, It's Not Whether They Win or Lose—But How Much the Sponsor Pays," *San Jose Mercury-News*, September 24, 1995.

Miki Turner, "Women in Sports: Playing for Pride," *Orange County Register*, October 31, 1994.

Ray Waddell, "Half of MLB's 28 Teams Keep Prices at '94 Levels," *Amusement Business*, May 29, 1995.

———, "NBA's Popularity, Salaries Cited for Fan Cost Increase," *Amusement Business*, December 6, 1993.

Joe Williams, "Women Who Coach Girls Declining," *Orlando Sentinel*, November 8, 1994.

Richard L. Worsnop, "The Business of Sports," *CQ Researcher*, February 10, 1995.

———, "College Sports," *CQ Researcher*, August 26, 1994.

Index

About the Author

Sarah Flowers is a writer and a librarian. She holds a B.A. from Kansas State University, an M.A. from the University of California, Berkeley, and an M.L.S. from San Jose State University. She is a librarian at the Morgan Hill Public Library in Morgan Hill, California, where she lives with her husband and their three sons. Her favorite sports are baseball, basketball, and tennis. She roots for the Kansas City Royals, the San Francisco Giants, women's basketball, and all the teams on which her sons play. This is her second book.

Picture Credits